LOVE

From the Jungle to the Divine

R. Stephen Lynch

Library of Congress Cataloging-in-Publication Data:

Lynch, R. Stephen
Love – From the Jungle to the Divine

Cover design: Michael Vito Tosto

For more information, visit the author's webpage:

Costaricacenterforjungianstudy.com

This book is dedicated to my daughter Caroline, who has taught me much more than I have her, to James Hollis, who generously shared his time and attention as I studied his powerful books, and to Yogi Liao Chian for his valuable editing and insight into Divine Love.

CONTENTS

PREFACE

This book was born out of the pain of failed romantic relationships that I have observed all around me my whole young life – my own, those of folks I know, and those of complete strangers whose tragedies are so great that they end up in the news and true crime books.

I wanted badly to understand why such relationships succeed or fail. What do partners bring into each relationship that either enhances or diminishes it over time? So, after my second divorce over ten years ago, I set out on a journey seeking to answer these questions. I found my own therapy sessions, my study of important contemporary psychological theories, and many conversations with wise men and women who have spent lifetimes studying these issues, thrilling!

Over time, it became abundantly clear to me: factors within us that most of us are not even aware of, powerful unconscious dynamics, drive modern-day human mating decisions... and determine whether they succeed or fail. I began to understand myself and others in a new and more powerful way. And I developed an intentionally simplistic way to understand youthful mating dynamics: the Jungle Equation. What compels me about the Jungle Equation is that the longer I have thought about this idea, the longer I have lived, and the more I experience, the more certain I have become of its simple verity.

I absolutely did not set out on my journey to write a book. Having neither advanced degrees in Psychology nor a collection of lectures and papers under my belt, nor any experience in counseling others. It just simply had not occurred to me.

Yet the insight I discovered trying to answer my own questions was so meaningful to me that I naturally wanted to tell everyone. Perhaps I could organize a seminar where folks came to hear directly from those authors and scholars that I had found so valuable. My early plans were quickly sidelined by the limitations imposed by the Covid pandemic. Still, I felt an urgency to share. So, that summer, I assembled a modest group of young folks closest to me and invited them to join me every Sunday afternoon for a couple of months whereby I introduced this valuable material to them. Some physically attended in my beach home in Maine and some attended virtually. I assigned readings and encouraged discussion of the material. Alas, it was great fun! Participants eagerly engaged and I felt I was doing something very important in their young lives. Fall came and folks departed my warm

Maine beach for their permanent residences, but not before our grand finale.

The last session was a live virtual group chat with noted scholar and author Dr. James Hollis, who by now was regularly gracing me with his valuable time, responding to my questions, and in some cases challenges, and who had become a mentor and source of great encouragement. Dr. Hollis has extraordinary skills, happily and lovingly sharing insights in an easily accessible manner, insights and ideas that can seem, at first hearing, complex and confusing.

A light went off in my head... I certainly could not write a scholarly psychology book but perhaps I could write a simple book. One that introduced important ideas about relationships and early mating in a fun and engaging manner. A book written in that wonderful manner in which Dr. Hollis had spoken. A book that did not have to be studied but could simply be read. A book that is meant to empower its readers, to invite them to stop blaming themselves, and to be a good news book.

We often blame ourselves for our failed relationships. Especially after 2 or 3 such experiences, we often feel we are the problem; we might ask ourselves "What is wrong with me?" The answer, my dear friends, is nothing is wrong with you! Broken hearts are a universal human experience. The next phase in your life is understanding what happened... consciousness, peace, self-love and more.

The good news is that motivated by the pain of early failures and armed with a capable mind we can learn a great deal about ourselves and others that will lead us into new relationships that are built on much stronger foundations, perhaps with the same partner, perhaps not. The task, however, requires one great commitment... a willingness and an ability to be brutally honest in our search for understanding ourselves, understanding our family and friends, and acknowledging our fear-based self-protective but ultimately self-defeating behavior and thoughts that are a constant demon tugging at our shirt sleeves, seeking attention and obeyance.

And more good news — surviving the pain of early romantic failures has many rewards: discovery of our soul's extraordinary resilience, self-love, an enhanced ability to love and forgive others, and, most importantly, an invitation to higher love, to blood love, loving friendships and, ultimately, Divine Love.

LOVE

From the Jungle to the Divine

1.

THE JUNGLE EQUATION

You know I've always been a dreamer
(Spent my life running round)
And it's so hard to change
Can't seem to settle down
But the dreams I've seen lately
Keep on turning out and burning out
and turning out the same
So put me on a highway
Show me a sign
Take it to the limit
One more time

"Take It to the Limit"
The Eagles

We've been conditioned to believe that we are not complete without that special someone who will magically make us complete.

There are vast vested interests dedicated to the perpetuation of harmful societal myths surrounding love, mating, and marriage. Diamond merchants, wedding planners, gift registries, and all sorts of bridal shower, rehearsal dinner, and honeymoon venues, divorce lawyers, and many other enterprises are dependent upon perpetuating the idea of the wonderful (and often expensive and very public) wedding day as a culmination of our search for our magical other.

Perhaps the strongest influence comes from family and friends. We see our peers one-by-one appear to find their magical other and hear our own family and friends urging us to seek that wonderful happy-ever-after day regardless of the unconfessed and hidden failures of their own mating decisions.

These forces and others make today's myth-based mating almost unavoidable when we are young and unwise and, sadly, sometimes when we are old and still unwise.

So, what is the Jungle Equation? Here it is:

Modern western culture, and in particular the pairing of young couples in short- and medium-term relationships, has nothing to do with love but rather is based entirely on commonly shared but unconscious, or certainly unconfessed, prehistoric, and primal desires of power and superficial sexual attraction.

Youthful mating nearly always manifests separative behavior, fear, and dualistic thinking and we are indeed in a jungle.

Jungle love is possessive (my wife or husband). It manifests dependence and selfish desires and is judgmental (when there is judgment, there is no real love). Jungle love sets expectations for the other and we want those expectations to be met. If the other meets my expectations, I love him/her; if he/she doesn't meet my expectations, then love is no longer there or turns into dislike or worse.

Jungle love does not accept the other as he or she is but wants the other to change or to be different and is not forgiving; elements of competition often arise.

However, Jungle love is dominant in western culture... it is a powerful force and totally survivable. In fact, it can be an important stepping stone to real love, as we will address in the latter chapters of this book.

But first, let's examine the power of the Jungle Equation.

Test this theory for yourself... consider the superficial, visual appearance of each partner in any medium-term (let's say 2 years +) relationship or marriage you encounter. You will find that visually attractive men are paired with visually attractive women and that less attractive men are paired with less attractive women. Where this is not the case you will see that the less attractive partner possesses dis-equal power in the form of money, fame, prestige, or other power manifestations.

This is the jungle equation; it is brutal, controversial, and almost universally true!

By the way, for simplicity, my examples assume a conventional one male, one female couple. The jungle equation applies equally to same-sex couples. I have also used the moniker girl and guy because this phenomenon occurs most clearly in young people under 35 years old or so.

If we rate visual attraction on a scale of 1-10 then a pairing of equally attractive people could be described as follows:

8 girl = 8 guy, or
2 girl = 2 guy

Or if a same sex relationship

8 girl = 8 girl, or
2 girl = 2 girl

Or

8 guy = 8 guy, or
2 guy = 2 guy

All are balanced.

If we rate a party's power in the form of a lot of money, a big house, a secure financial future, family money, fame, or other forms of power on a scale of 1-10, then some relationships can be described as follows:

8 girl = 3 guy with 5 power, it balances to...
8 girl = 8 guy

Or it could be the other way around...

8 guy = 3 girl with 5 power
8 guy = 8 girl

Or if a same sex relationship

8 girl = 3 girl with 5 power, it balances to...
8 girl = 8 girl

Or it could be the other way around...

8 guy = 3 guy with 5 power, it balances to...
8 guy = 8 guy

What I would argue is that you will never see, and I mean

never, an early life medium-term relationship that violates the Jungle Equation like:

8 girl = 3 guy with no power, or vice versa.

When you do see it, it is because it won't last, or the balancing power score is just not visible... but it is there. Some young folks call a brief exception a "Sympathy Kiss" to use an expression that's less crude than the one I've heard.

So, all early relationships begin with a balanced Jungle Equation... where's the problem you might ask?

Well, the problem is that over time, maybe quickly, maybe over several years, every couple's Jungle Equation is very likely to be thrown substantially and permanently out of balance. One very common example is the happy couple with a balanced equation. Over time they both age and become less attractive. But also, over time he may become very rich, famous, or powerful in other ways beyond attractiveness while she just gets old. As the cruel joke goes, he trades in his fifty-year-old for two 25's!

Of course, it may be the other way around... she may become very rich, famous, or powerful in other ways beyond attractiveness while he becomes a couch potato.

Another common pattern that cracks the Jungle Equation

balance is when much of her side of the equation is her beauty while his is big bucks. She ages well and keeps her side of the equation strong, but business events occur that cost him his wealth. What happens? You know! She dumps him for another rich guy.

I invite readers to now set this book aside and think of all the ways you have seen or experienced the breaking of a previously aligned Jungle Equation.

Now, see how common this is? So, the problem with initial mating in obeyance to the Jungle Equation is that it has every possibility of falling apart over time with all the ensuing pain and damage to children, extended family, and others around the couple, or the relationship may grow into one the manifests a more permeant but less thrilling love, routed in respect and common goals and values.

As I wrote in the Preface to this book: Importantly, we often blame ourselves for our early failed relationships. Especially after two or three such experiences, we often feel we are the problem; we might ask ourselves "What is wrong with me?" The answer, my dear friends, is nothing is wrong with you! Broken hearts are a universal human experience. The next phase in your life is understanding what happened… consciousness and self-love.

If one is fortunate enough at a young age to have read

books like this or to have been taught wisely by parents, therapists, or other elders, or simply by the grace of God, he or she may be conscious enough to avoid choosing a mate simply because the Jungle Equation is currently balanced. Sadly, these are the exceptions. When I think about, maybe, 10 young couples that I think I know I would say perhaps 2 possess qualities that transcend the brutal equation.

I say "think I know" because it is impossible to know what's really going on between people. Many couples are living unhappy lives with broken Equations, but they bang on, presenting a brave, false façade.

And some few, simply with good luck, the grace of God, or heightened consciousness and wisdom early on can avoid the problems of early obeyance of the mandates of the Jungle Equation.

However, there are forces at work within us from even before birth that compound the likelihood of mating disaster in the first half of life. We'll explore these forces in the following chapter.

2.

THE HIDDEN FORCES AT WORK WITHIN US

I am an old woman
Named after my mother
My old man's another
Child that's grown old

If dreams were thunder
And lightning was desire
This old house would have burnt down
A long time ago

"Angel From Montgomery"
John Prine

As James Hollis so clearly wrote, life begins traumatically... we are born! No one fully recovers from this first assault. We are thrust from our divine ocean into a world where we are surrounded by more powerful people, and we no longer always get what we want.

Our early child wounding is a universal experience. Those

fortunate to be surrounded by loving thoughtful parents may experience less trauma while others more, but we are all deeply wounded in our early life.

One common example is the wounding of the firstborn child. "In spite of sharing genes and environments, siblings are often not as similar in nature as one might think. But where do differences come from? Alfred Adler, a 19th- and early 20th-century Austrian psychotherapist, suspected that birth order leads to differences in siblings. Wounding occurs to the firstborn because they don't have to share their parents for years and are essentially dethroned once a sibling comes along. Adler considered firstborns to be neurotic, dutiful, and conservative.[1]

American psychologist Frank J. Sulloway, who, in the mid-1990s, combed history books for leading figures who were firstborns and rebellious ones who were born later, saw a similar trend. Among the later borns, he found lateral thinkers and revolutionaries, such as Charles Darwin, Karl Marx, and Mahatma Gandhi. But among firstborns, he discovered leaders such as Joseph Stalin and Benito Mussolini. His explanation? Every child occupies a certain niche within the family and then uses his or her own strategies to master life. Firstborn and single children have less reason to quarrel with the status quo and identify more strongly with the worldview of their fathers and mothers. Younger siblings are less sure of their parents' view and therefore more often choose alternative paths in life.

Sadly, firstborns can often go through life being bossy, desperately seeking control over others, and repeatedly trying and failing to reassert their lost authoritative position. They can, however, sometimes become conscious of their internal landscape and more mature.

James Hollis writes:

> The power of these primal, formative experiences in programing our sense of self, our sense of the world 'out there,' and how we are to relate to it can hardly be overemphasized. In the initial years of our life – unsupported by the development of an ego that surveys the world and its alternatives, learns parallel possibilities, learns to differentiate cause and effect better – we all are limited to a modality of experiencing, which anthropologists and archetypal psychologists call 'magical thinking'." Magical thinking results from an insufficient ability to differentiate self and world. The child concludes that "The world is an encoded message to me, a statement about me, about how I am valued, and how I am to comport myself." Another way of putting this is "I am what happens to me, a state-

> ment about me." Decades later we may begin to differentiate better. We learn that Mother's anger, or Dad's aloofness... was the limitation of Another and not about ourselves at all. But this recognition comes late in life, if at all, and after many turns and returns.[2]

Hollis addresses two general categories of our early existential trauma, the wound of Overwhelment and the wound of Insufficiency or Abandonment. Several specific unconscious strategies are typically chosen in each case. Of course, no one fits cleanly into any category. Rather, I have come to believe that we are all a mix of each of these with different weightings.[3]

The wound of Overwhelment is our realization of our powerlessness whether at the hand of overbearing parents, poverty, biological impairment, or other circumstances. Some of the most common strategies chosen by those reacting to the experience of the wound of Overwhelment include:

— Evasion... i.e., retreating, avoiding, procrastinating, and denying

— Control, i.e., get in control of our environment before it controls us

— Give them what they want... or Codependence

The wound of Insufficiency or Abandonment is the feeling that when we do not get all we want as infants it is because we are not worthy of such love. Even children of healthy loving parents may experience this although to a lesser degree. Some of the most common strategies chosen by those reacting to the experience of the wound of Insufficiency or Abandonment include:

— Hiding, avoiding risks, and self-sabotage

— Overcompensating by seeking wealth, power, fame, beauty, etc.

— Anxiously and obsessively seeking the assurance of others

So, we all have suffered, to some degree or other, childhood wounds and the necessary and appropriate building up of strategies to protect ourselves. These strategies define what some call our provisional personality as distinct from our true self which might emerge later in life when we feel safer and or when the provisional tools so necessary in our youth betray us as adults. However, the provisional tools can be very effective in early childhood and right through adolescence and early adulthood.

So, you might ask, what does this have to do with early mating decisions and the Jungle Equation?

I would suggest that the early childhood wounding dynamic influences early mating decisions and the potential for success or failure in two primary ways.

First, it is exactly these unconscious strategies and tools that we develop to implement them that are the primary energy building up the "assets" that populate our side of the Jungle Equation!

Among other tools we may finely hone in order to enhance our side of the Equation are:

Attractiveness Tools

1. Physical beauty (which can be very much a matter of choice)
2. Seductiveness and other allurement tools
3. Humor
4. Sarcasm
5. Wit
6. Charm

Power Tools

1. Knowledge
2. Commitment and hard work
3. Manipulation skills
4. Deceit and cheating skills
5. Disguises

By early adulthood, we generally know the tools we have available to maximize our side of the Equation, but we are not yet conscious of the early childhood wounding that compelled their creation nor their long-term limitations.

All is well when the Jungle Equation is in balance… we are a "Power Couple." But as the Equation inevitably starts to fall out of balance, our old strategies and tools, our "old map" that guided us well in the past, comes into play again, but it does not work anymore!

The old map will first be used to try to fix, manage or just tolerate our current broken relationship.

Tragically, some couples bang on together forever in broken, loveless relationships. More tragically, most find another mate with another currently balanced Equation.

Those in the state of perpetually finding and failing into new relationships should ask themselves, "What was the one common thing in all my failed relationships?" Answer: You!

Unless and until we become conscious of the elements of our old map, why we had to create it, why it worked well for a while, and why it no longer works, we will spend our life in one of two sad states: tolerating a meaningless relationship or perpetually seeking a new one with old maps.

The early childhood wounding dynamic influences early relationships and their potential for success or failure in a second important way. The necessary and appropriate strategies we all construct to protect ourselves, the elements of our young provisional personalities, also serve as ego boundaries. We feel safer and more comfortable armed with these strong, seemingly self-protective tools. However, they also serve to limit or block intimacy with others. One cannot simultaneously manifest all the power of our boundaries while revealing the pain, fear, and vulnerability so necessary for true connection with our fellow human beings.

However, when young adults, flush with surging sexual energy and urgencies driven by a prehistoric and genetic drive to procreate, meet someone who they perceive to have an equal Jungle Equation, the stage is often set for the sudden, complete, and mutual dismantling of all ego boundaries.

This phenomenon is one of the most wonderful and yet often most misleading of all human experiences... Falling in Love!

3.

FALLING IN LOVE

I took my love, took it down
I climbed a mountain, and I turned around
And I saw my reflection in the snow-covered hills
'Til a landslide brought me down

Oh, mirror in the sky, what is love?
Can the child within my heart rise above?
Can I sail through the changing ocean tides?
Can I handle the seasons of my life?

"Landslide"
Stevie Nicks

I love margaritas. I love my garden. I love my kids. I love you. The word love is a very ambiguous and confusing word in the English language. This ambiguity belies the confusion in our "love" relationships in contemporary Western culture. The "love" involved in Falling in Love is not true love any more than the love involved in the pleasure from our margaritas. More advanced cultures have many words for the various types and conditions of "love." In Sanskrit, for example, there are over seventy words for love.

M. Scott Peck writes:

> Of all the misconceptions about love the most powerful and pervasive is the belief that 'falling in love' is love or at least one of the manifestations of love. It is a potent misconception, because falling in love is subjectively experienced in a very powerful fashion as an experience of love. When a person falls in love what he or she certainly feels is 'I love him' or 'I love her.' But two problems are immediately apparent. The first is that the experience of falling in love is specifically a sex-link erotic experience. We do not fall in love with our children even though we may love them very deeply. We do not fall in love with friends of the same sex – unless we are homosexually oriented-even though we may care for them greatly. We fall in love only when we are consciously or unconsciously sexually motivated. The second problem is that the experience of falling in love is invariably temporary. No matter whom we fall in love with, we sooner or later fall out of love if the relationship continues long enough.[4]

As noted in the previous chapter, while we feel safer and more comfortable armed with our ego boundaries they also serve to limit or block intimacy with others. Living solely and always with such walls is ultimately a very lonely experience. So, when we Fall in Love and dismantle our walls, we free ourselves from ourselves. We open ourselves up to our beloved, we feel we will never be lonely again, that this feeling will last forever, and we are ecstatic. Sadly, it is an illusion.

It's an illusion that greatly serves our collective unconscious and I would say our genetically imprinted drive to procreate. In earlier times having many babies may have been necessary for the survival of the human species. Today the species is more at risk for too many babies, too little self-knowledge, too little self-love, and too little love of our fellow travelers.

Furthermore, it is an illusion supported and promoted by many cultural factors. It is a common theme of many childhood fairy tales, the idea that one day we will meet our prince or princess, the one and only for us, and live happily ever after. Many popular songs and movies suggest this illusion is not an illusion.

And, as noted previously, there are vast vested interests dedicated to the perpetuation of harmful societal myths surrounding love, mating, and marriage. Diamond merchants, wedding planners, gift registries, and all sorts of bridal shower, rehearsal dinner, and honeymoon venues, divorce lawyers, and many other enterprises are dependent upon perpetuating the idea of the wonderful (and expensive and often very public) wedding day as a culmination of our search for our magical other.

But if you're reading this book, you may already be growing skeptical of this myth, this illusion... and you should thank your higher powers for that.

Peck further writes:

> Just as reality intrudes upon the two-year-old's fantasy of omnipotence so does reality intrude upon the fantastic unity of the couple who have fallen in love. Sooner or later, in response to the problems of daily living, individuality will reassert itself. He wants to have sex, she doesn't. He wants to put money in the bank, she wants to buy a new dishwasher. She wants to talk about her job, he wants to talk about his. She doesn't like his friends; he doesn't like hers. So, both of them, in the privacy of their hearts, begin to come to the sickening realization that they are not one with the beloved, that the beloved has and will continue to have his or her own desires, tastes, prejudices and timing difference from the other's. One by one, gradually, or suddenly, they fall out of love. Once again, they are two separate individuals. At this point they begin either to dissolve ties of relationship or to initiate the work of real loving.[5]

4.

WHAT IS REAL LOVE?

The greatest poem ever known
Is one all poets have outgrown
The poetry, innate, untold
Of being only four years old

Still young enough to be a part
Of Nature's great impulsive heart
Born comrade of bird, beast, and tree
And unselfconscious as the bee

And yet with lovely reason skilled
Each day new paradise to build
Elate explorer of each sense
Without dismay, without pretense!

In your unstained transparent eyes
There is no conscience, no surprise
Life's queer conundrums you accept
Your strange divinity still kept

Being, that now absorbs you, all
Harmonious, unit, integral

Will shred into perplexing bits
Oh, contradictions of the wits!

And Life, that sets all things in rhyme
may make you poet, too, in time
But there were days, O tender elf
When you were Poetry itself!

"To a Child"
Christopher Morley

So, this brings us to a big question... what is real love? Many pages and volumes have been written by wise men and women such as Hollis, Peck, Jung, McGehee, and Bradshaw, to name a few.

About ten years ago I had an experience with my only child that was a real awakening. She had fallen in love for the first time. The young man was a college classmate and her age, but from a different country with a very different and patriarchal culture. She greatly valued this relationship, and I was open-minded and happy to get to know him.

So, the three of us had an introductory lunch and I was horrified. This man was domineering and controlling of my daughter and clearly saw me as a threat to his dominion over her. I did my best to conceal my true feelings and try to find common ground, but the mutual distrust was heavy in the air.

When he left, I told my daughter why I thought this was not a good relationship for her. She had to return to work, and we agreed to chat that evening.

That evening we went for a long walk together. She was consumed with anger and fear. How could I jeopardize one of the most important things in her life? Maybe he perceived how I felt and would leave her. Maybe he would find out later and leave her.

Of course, my daughter knows me very well. She knows all my faults and limitations. She attacked me accurately for all these things. I spoke very little as she vented for over an hour. When we got home, I went to bed and, to my surprise, I felt, amongst all this turmoil and acrimony, totally peaceful! I did not know why, and I fell asleep.

In the morning she woke me up in tears… "Dad, I am so sorry. I feel terrible about all the things I said to you yesterday. I didn't mean it; I was just afraid that you would scare him away."

I said, "Dear, oddly, your words, as accurate of my flaws as they were, did not hurt me a bit! I was just hoping that your venting might bring you some relief. I love you and will support you in whatever decisions you make."

And I felt and meant every one of those spontaneous, from-the-heart, words! This was a crash course in real love between two humans... and I wondered how might one seek or strive to create this wonderful condition?

Perhaps I had it easy. My daughter evidenced a sweet and good nature from an early age, notwithstanding a divorce and co-parenting arrangements from three years old on. She looks like me, is smart and kind and I believe we possess a lot of common genetics. I naturally loved her. I loved spending hours on the floor playing with our little farm animals together, constructing stories about their school days (under the sofa) and their bus ride to and from. We watched the same fun movies over and over to the point that we would sing the songs and speak the key lines together as we watched. My love flowed naturally and endlessly right up until today. This is a kind of real love that sometimes, not always, arises between parents and children, between siblings, and sometimes other family members. I call this "blood love." It does also occur between non-blood relations, though this is even more rare.

Of course, as my daughter grew up there were the normal trials and tribulations regarding school, friends, and the other aspects of an unfolding life. It was not always fun. I worried a lot about her safety, health, and happiness as most parents do. My love for her hurt at times and required me to set aside other things in my life to attend to her. But I did it unquestionably; naturally. And so, this natural blood love was present during that long walk and talk and is endless.

However, I have come to believe that a second condition is necessary for real love, whether among family members or not and that is self-love. Without self-love and the related self-forgiveness that it leads to, her hurtful words would have hurt. They did not.

It took me forty years before I forgive myself for all my flaws and came to understand that I was GOOD... certainly not perfect, but a good guy, worthy of love. This happened suddenly within two years of my daughter's birth and was a necessary condition for my love for her.

Interestingly, while setting the stage for blood love, this experience also began to reveal to me more clearly the third, and ultimate, kind of love in the world... Divine Love... but more about this later in the book.

As a necessary condition to being truly loving to others, self-love is not self-indulgent, but rather, it's a great gift you may give the world. How one achieves self-love and why some live their whole lives without it remains largely a mystery to me. I only know what happened to me, so I'll ask your indulgence for one more autobiographical snippet of my life.

I graduated from a middle-class American public High School in East Hartford, Connecticut at the top of my Class and I was miserable. I was the class brain who couldn't get a date for the Prom.

I was funny looking, played no sports, and was in great pain. I had also developed a provisional personality, a strategy to make up for all that I lacked, and that was academic excellence. And, because of my top grades in high school, I was one of only a few kids who were accepted into a private College, and, in my case, it was a very elite New England College called Bowdoin College, in Maine.

At Bowdoin I had even more books and a better library, and, as it was the dawn of the computer age, I had access to one of the first computers in New England. 600 students shared 1 computer, so you signed up days in advance for your 1-hour slot... except Saturday Night! Starting around 7pm no one wanted to use the computer, so I had it all to myself till the early morning hours, what a treat!

So, this thing of mine, loving to study, loving to learn, and escaping from the pain of socializing continued and led me to a undergraduate degree in economics and a master's degree in finance, all near the top of my class at elite colleges, and to make a long story short, shy, nerdy twenty-year-old Steve ends up an Investment Banker in a Manhattan Penthouse with beautiful clothes and cars and pretty girlfriends. I built a little estate an hour and a half north of the city for the weekends. And married I the prettiest girl I could get, and we soon had our wonderful daughter.

This was a classic case of building up walls and living a compensatory, provisional personality, and therefore I was miserable inside. This situation could have lasted a lifetime. That's why I now believe there was some great benevolent and transcendent force at work when it all fell apart. By then I owned and ran my own financial advisory firm, with bigger risks than working for others but bigger returns too.

And my company started to struggle, debts piled up, my marriage quickly failed, and I lost my big house. I once again was miserable and self-loathing. I blamed myself completely for all my troubles. So I decided to take a totally brutal and honest look at myself, and I saw what a flawed person I had become.

I was not shy anymore I was cocky, and very proud of all the stuff I had. I had built a house with big strong walls on a very weak foundation. I had spent the last 20 years trying to prove that I am OK. If I lose it all and my beautiful wife, I'll be nothing again. I blamed myself for all of it and lived in fear and despair for about a year.

Then, one Saturday night around 3am, I awoke suddenly

and received a clear and direct message! The message was "Steve, pick yourself up! Do not despair! You are a good guy! You were born a good guy, you still are a good guy, and you will always be even if you have no beautiful wife, no fancy cars, no big house... you still have you... and me."

Suddenly, the weight of the world was lifted off my shoulders. I was utterly overwhelmed with thanks and relief. I got into my car and drove to my little church in the countryside, sat in the front row, and cried and prayed. I drove home as the sun rose.

What an unlikely, extraordinary experience! No science or math book could explain this. A Divine power had suddenly and unambiguously saved my life. And I've been living life ever since with the Divine blessing of self-love. To be clear, I continued to mess up sometimes, but I ask myself why in a constructive way without negative self-judgment.

Perhaps I was lucky again... all did was allow myself to be miserable. Perhaps, more improbably, I decided to be brutally honest with myself about myself. I think this was key. And I abandoned all my walls and felt empty and afraid, meek... between worlds, the old self was dead, but I could not see the new. I believe that this condition is necessary for true growth. This idea is wonderfully expressed in these lines from "Amazing Grace":

> Twas grace that taught my heart to fear, and Grace my fear relieved.

So, I have come to know that self-love and self-forgiveness is a necessary condition for real love of others. Without self-love my daughter's critical words to me on that fateful walk would have hurt... but they did not. Without self-love, I would have focused more on defending or explaining or justifying myself... but I did not. I was fully present in her suffering and my ability to relieve it.

In 1978 Scott Peck offered up a definition of real love that seems as good as any to me:

> Love is the will to extend oneself for the purpose of nurturing one's own or another's spiritual growth.

Peck understood that extending oneself means volunteering to endure necessary pain and suffering as we undertake unnatural behaviors that include delaying gratification, assuming full responsibility for our lives and our actions, and a total and utter commitment to truth, both with others and with ourselves. And most importantly, as Peck noted, *"Love is **not** a feeling"* Sadly, contemporary western culture sends us just the opposite message.

So, let's summarize. We've discussed and explored Jungle Love which is also called romantic love, eros love, and other names. This kind of love never lasts and is ego-centric, but the relationship may grow into one that manifests a more permanent but less thrilling love, routed in respect, common goals, and common values.

Then we discussed blood love which is one circumstance for the emergence of the love of others. And I suggested that self-love was a necessary precondition for the love of others, blood or otherwise.

McGahee writes:

> Friendship, that is, the love between two friends, may be the most undervalued kind of love in our culture. The very idea of not having a friend or a support system, of not having brothers and sisters who can hold our hand, be present with us in dark places and celebrate joyous occasions with us, is unthinkable. So Phila, or brotherly love like the City of Philadelphia, is the love that Jung called kinship...[6]

Now let's turn to the most wonderous and difficult to describe love of all... Divine Love.

5.

DIVINE LOVE

There's a love that's divine
And it's yours and it's mine
Like the sun

"Have I Told You Lately That I Love You?"
Van Morrison

My first clear encounter with the Divine was that Saturday night at the age of forty-three when I was completely miserable and in a state of self-loathing for months. Then one night, I awoke around 3am and suddenly received a clear, direct message! As mentioned previously, the message was this: "Steve, pick yourself up! Do not despair! You are a good guy! You were born a good guy, you still are a good guy, and you will always be even if you have no beautiful wife, no fancy cars, no big house... you still have you... and me." The absolute clarity and verity of this message changed my life forever.

While this was my first explicit, undeniable encounter with Divine Love, I have since had others and I have come to understand that this force has guided me and protected me my entire life... and will continue to do so!

Various names have been given to what I'm calling Divine Love, including "The Creator," "God," "Jesus," "Grace," and "Higher Power," to name just a few. My reading and study have led me to believe that the name we choose does not really matter because all are an attempt to name the same thing. One of the many things these concepts have in common is that many find that their encounters or experiences with them are impossible to describe with words. Divine love is irrationally blissful, transcendent of thought and words, and exists far from any other human experience or knowledge. Scholars recognize this as the reason that the story of Jesus, just one of many manifestations of Divine love, is told in myths and legends... stories that can't be true from any physical or rational human point of view but serve as metaphors or hints at what the observer experienced. Many important mythical themes remain central to the story of Jesus such as we find in John 6:1-14, which tells how Jesus and his disciples fed five thousand people with "five small barley loaves and two small fish" or the miracle of Jesus walking on the water, or on the sea, as depicted in three of the Gospels; Matthew, Mark, and John.

While some argue that the use of myths and metaphor to describe Jesus evidences that the stories of Jesus and other manifestations of Divine Love are apocryphal, more, such as

Carl Jung, Joseph Campbell, and C. S. Lewis recognize that the use of myth and metaphor enhances the credibility of Divine Love encounters that can't be described with familiar thought or rational, words. Jung believed that myths are expressions of important collective human truths. C S Lewis wrote, "The value of the myth is that it takes all the things we know and restores to them the rich significance which has been hidden by 'the veil of familiarity.'"[7]

One very common type of encounter with Divine Love has been described in very similar ways by many... the blissful merging with the white light during near-death experiences. These wonderful experiences of merging with the white light occur during bardo, the state of existence intermediate between two lives on earth. Originally a Tibetan concept, bardo occurs after death and before one's next birth, when one's consciousness is not connected with a physical body. At this time, one experiences a variety of phenomena including the universal accounts of merging with the blissful white light. Accounts of near-death experiences are remarkably consistent including intensely vivid memories involving bodily sensations that give a strong impression of being more real than memories of true events. The content of those experiences always includes memories of one's life "flashing before the eyes," the sensation of leaving the body and blissfully merging with the white light, feeling profoundly connected to something universal.

This surely is an encounter with Divine Love. Fortunately, we do not have to wait for the end of our physical lives the encounter Divine Love. It can happen to anyone at any time spontaneously and often. While Divine Love is unconditional, my own experience is that are things we might do to encourage and recognize such encounters.

In my case, I believe that, as previously discussed, my first encounter at the age of forty-three was facilitated by my mental and spiritual state at the time. At that time, I had decided to take a totally brutal and honest look at myself, and I saw what a flawed person I had become. I was cocky, and very proud of all the stuff I had. I had built a house with big strong walls on a very weak foundation. I had spent the last twenty years trying to prove that I wasn't the small, insecure person I felt like inside. My business and my marriage were failing, and I blamed myself for all of it and lived in fear and despair for about a year. I felt lost and powerless. While this condition surely isn't necessary, for Divine Love is unconditional, I believe it helped. This idea, I believe, is what lies behind one of the so-called Beatitudes found in Matthew 5: 5: "Blessed are the meek: for they shall inherit the earth." The word meek in this case is a mental attitude; a combination of open-mindedness and acknowledged powerless. The earth that is inherited is not an earth of things but of inner peace.

A final note on Divine Love... I believe we often have encounters with the divine and do not recognize it. Think about the times in your life when things went wrong, only later to understand such failures as a blessing or good luck. Or think about times when, looking back, you see you were at great physical, financial, or spiritual risk, and yet you survived and prospered beyond reason. Or think about times when someone came into your life just at the right moment. Knowing that we are surrounded by Divine Love, even if we have not had an overwhelmingly transformative encounter yet, may help us realize that we have already experienced Divine Love, just without the spiritual thunder and lighting.

6.

WHAT ARE WE TO DO? SIX SUGGESTIONS

As you may have guessed by now, I have fallen in love several times and I am the wiser for it. I hope all of us fall in love at least once so that we might be invited to a higher consciousness when eros love inevitably disappoints.

And I must not claim any kind of higher wisdom. I spent the first half of my life embraced by unconsciousness and trying to prove that I was not the small, frightened person that I felt I was inside. This is common, and the energy we put into such projects can yield great things such as money and power...but not happiness.

So, what do I have to recommend?

First and **foremost**: My young friends, I repeat a third time, do not blame yourself for failed relationships, nothing is wrong with you! Broken hearts are a universal human experience. The next phase in your life is understanding what happened... consciousness, peace, self-love, and an invitation to perceive and engage with the Divine Love that surrounds you at all times.

"Heartbreak asks from us to be present to our suffering; it asks that we learn about ourselves and our personal history, and that we connect with our soul to find our path. Heartbreak raises our awareness of what it means to be human. More specifically, we learn to know ourselves intimately.

While dealing with pain and grief we gradually become aware of our defenses against it. Often, these defenses are our fear of suffering, the unknown, and the fear of listening to the soul's demands to walk our unique path.

But, when we learn to face our fears, let go and surrender, we learn to evolve. We gain strength and experience more love. In addition, new ways can come into being. That is the transformative potential in heartbreak. Overall, the invitation in heartbreak is to love more deeply."[8]

Second: Realize that everyone's life involves suffering. I would suggest that we should seek a meaningful life and happiness will follow. When in pain, understand that it will enlarge you if you face it head on.

This approach invites you to see your burdens and hardships as an invitation to deeper consciousness. Your soul has a higher agenda. When faced, each of these difficult tasks can enrich your life. You become more adaptable and tap into strengths of character. You align with your soul's wisdom. This will help you get unstuck and build personal authority.

As Shakespeare's Polonius said, "to thine own self be true." We may all need to fake it sometimes on the outside, but not to ourselves.

Third: Don't compare your insides to others' outsides. Meaning when we are troubled with our current relationship, we often look at other couples that look happy and in love. It is an illusion... we all put up a grand image for the public, but outsiders have no idea what the true condition of our relationship is.

Fourth: Please know that we are all divine, with all our scars and imperfections there is a higher power full of love for us all that is waiting for us to connect. Meditate, take deep breaths, and learn to forgive and love yourself... everything else will flow from that.

Fifth: Practice the conditions that may encourage divine encounters or at least allow us to recognize them when they do occur. Specifically, privately allow yourself to feel lost and powerless, to be spiritually meek, and open to the new you. In addition, there is a self-empowerment experiential tool that I have personally experienced with great benefits... guided imagery or, its milder cousin, guided meditation. This requires a skilled guide which can be hard but not impossible to find. In my case, in a darkened room with relaxing music, lying on my back after deep breathes, I was walked through the "junkyard" of my life to date all the way back to the day I was born: a perfect, divine child, as we all are born. It was another overwhelming, wonderful encounter with Divine Love for me.

Sixth: Seek wisdom from books. Of course, I mean classic books written by Hollis, Peck, McGehee, and Bradshaw, to name a few. I have included references in the Abbreviated Bibliography in the back of this book.

NOTES

1: "Does Birth Order Affect Personality?" Corinna Hartmann and Sara Goudarzi, Scientific American, August 8, 2019

2: Hollis, James. Finding Meaning in the Second Half of Life: How to Finally, Really Grow Up. Page 47. New York, Gotham Books, 2006.

3: Hollis, James. Finding Meaning in the Second Half of Life: How to Finally, Really Grow Up. Page 49. New York, Gotham Books, 2006.

4: Peck, M. Scott. The Road Less Traveled: A New Psychology of Love, Traditional Values and Spiritual Growth. Page 84. New York, Touchstone, 1978.

5: Peck, M. Scott. The Road Less Traveled : A New Psychology of Love, Traditional Values and Spiritual Growth. New York, Touchstone, 1978.

6: McGehee, J. Pittnam. The Paradox of Love. Houston, Tx, Bright Sky Press, 2011.

7: Lewis, C.S. On Stories: And Other Essays on Literature. Cambridge Ma, Harvard Press, 2002

8: Akke-Jeanne Klerk "Heartbreak and its Invitations" JungPlatform Course, 2022

ABBREVIATED BIBLIOGRAPHY

Bradshaw, John. *Home Coming: Reclaiming and Championing Your Inner Child*. London, Piatkus, 1990.

Hollis, James. *Finding Meaning in the Second Half of Life: How to Finally, Really Grow Up*. New York, Gotham Books, 2006.

Hollis, James. *Living between Worlds: Finding Personal Resilience in Changing Times*. Boulder, Co, Sounds True, 2020.

Hollis, James. *The Eden Project: In Search of the Magical Other*. Toronto, Ont., Inner City Books, 1998.

McGehee, J. Pittnam. The Paradox of Love. Houston, Tx, Bright Sky Press, 2011.

Peck, M. Scott. *Further along the Road Less Travelled: Wisdom for the Journey towards Spiritual Growth: New York, Simon and Schuster, 1998*

Peck, M. Scott. *The Road Less Traveled: A New Psychology of Love, Traditional Values and Spiritual Growth.* New York, Touchstone, 1978.

www.ingramcontent.com/pod-product-compliance
Lightning Source LLC
LaVergne TN
LVHW091236150826
845673LV00003B/1166

* 9 7 9 8 3 6 6 6 8 1 8 1 0 *